LE CORDON BLEU

HOME COLLECTION

·WINTER·

MURDOCH BOOKS®

Sydney • London • Vancouver • New York

contents

4
Warm oyster mushroom salad

6
Clear borscht with piroshki

8
Pot-au-feu

10
Trout flans with chive and lemon sauce

12
Scallops dieppoise

14
Consommé with chicken quenelles

16
Country-style terrine

18
Beef Wellington

20
Lamb medallions with redcurrant sauce

22
Pork chops with sage

24
Roasted duck with turnips

26
Blanquette of lamb in garlic cream

28
Roast beef and Yorkshire puddings

30
Salmon, leek and potato gratin

32
Normandy pork

34
Roasted lamb with vegetables

36
Steak and kidney pudding

38
Stuffed veal escalopes

40
Lamb stew with potatoes

42
Treacle and almond tart

44
Rhubarb and ginger pudding with caramel sauce

46
Fruit tarts with vanilla syrup

48
Steamed orange pudding

50
Chocolate and chestnut terrine

52
Pears poached in red wine

54
Baked rice pudding

56
Fresh fruit mincemeat tart

58
Apple fritters

60
Apple meringues with raspberry coulis

62
Chef's techniques

recipe ratings ❖ *easy* ❖❖ *a little more care needed* ❖❖❖ *more care needed*

Warm oyster mushroom salad

Simple to prepare, this salad is nevertheless layered with texture and flavour. Warm, succulent oyster mushrooms nestle on a bed of crisp lettuce, doused with vinaigrette and sprinkled with celeriac chips, to make an unusual starter or an excellent light luncheon dish.

*Preparation time **20 minutes***
*Total cooking time **20 minutes***
Serves 4–6

¹/₂ celeriac
a few drops of lemon juice
400 g (12³/4 oz) oyster mushrooms
200 g (6¹/2 oz) mixed salad leaves
25 ml (³/4 fl oz) balsamic vinegar
115 ml (3³/4 fl oz) good-quality olive oil
oil, for deep-frying
4 French shallots, chopped

1 Peel the celeriac and cut into thin, even slices, placing them in a bowl of cold water with lemon juice added. Set aside until ready to use.

2 Cut the mushrooms into large, bite-size pieces. Wash the salad leaves, then drain them and dry on tea towels or in a salad-spinner. Refrigerate to keep crisp.

3 To make the vinaigrette, place the vinegar into a bowl with some salt and pepper and whisk together. Slowly add 100 ml (3¹/4 fl oz) of the oil in a steady stream, whisking continuously to form an emulsion. If the vinaigrette is too sharp, whisk in a little more oil.

4 Preheat a deep-fat fryer or deep pan, one-third full of oil, to 185°C (375°F). Test the temperature by adding a single drained and dried celeriac slice: if the oil bubbles vigorously around the chip, the oil is ready.

5 Drain and dry the celeriac slices thoroughly. Place a quarter of the celeriac slices into a wire basket and lower the basket into the oil. Cook the slices for about 3 minutes, or until golden and crisp, stirring occasionally to encourage even colouring. Remove and drain on crumpled paper towels. Repeat in batches with the remaining slices. Sprinkle the drained chips with salt while they are still warm.

6 Heat the remaining olive oil in a deep frying pan, add the shallots and cook gently, without colouring, until soft and transparent. Increase the heat to medium, add the mushrooms and toss quickly for 6–8 minutes.

7 To assemble the salad, toss the salad leaves with the vinaigrette and arrange on serving plates. Spoon on the mushroom and shallot mixture and sprinkle with celeriac chips. Serve at once, while the mushrooms are still warm.

Clear borscht with piroshki

There are many variations of this popular Eastern European soup, yet the ingredient that always imparts its colour is beetroot. This soup is very light and is served with piroshki: Russian potato and onion turnovers.

*Preparation time **1 hour + 45 minutes standing
+ 1 hour refrigeration***
*Total cooking time **1 hour***
*Serves **4–6***

PIROSHKI

135 g (4¹/₂ oz) plain flour
7 g (¹/₄ oz) fresh yeast or 14 g (¹/₂ oz) dried yeast
2 tablespoons warm milk
I egg, beaten
45 g (1¹/₂ oz) unsalted butter, at room temperature
200 g (6¹/₂ oz) potatoes
I small onion, finely diced
I egg, beaten
oil, for deep-frying

BORSCHT

1.25 litres brown stock (see page 63)
**2 beetroots, about 275 g (9 oz) each, peeled and
    coarsely grated**
2 egg whites
I tablespoon salt
¹/₂ teaspoon sugar
2 tablespoons lemon juice
snipped fresh chives, to garnish

1 To make the piroshki dough, sift the flour and a pinch of salt into a bowl. Mix the yeast with the milk and stir until liquid. Pour the milk into the beaten egg, then add the mixture to the flour and bring together to a soft, sticky dough. Beat for 1 minute, or until smooth, then work in 15 g (¹/₂ oz) of the butter until well combined. Cover with plastic wrap and leave in a warm place to rise for 30 minutes. Punch down the dough and chill for at least 1 hour, or overnight.

2 To make the piroshki filling, peel the potatoes and place in a large pan of salted water. Bring to the boil, then reduce the heat and simmer for 20–25 minutes, or until tender to the point of a knife. Drain the potato, cut into small cubes and set aside. Melt the remaining butter in a small pan, add the onion, then cover and cook gently for 5 minutes, or until soft. Increase the heat to medium, uncover the pan and cook for 2–3 minutes, or until a light golden brown. Remove from the heat, stir in the potato cubes and season well with salt and freshly ground pepper. Allow to cool.

3 To make the borscht, place the stock, beetroot, egg whites, salt, sugar, lemon juice and some finely ground black pepper in a large pan. Heat gently, whisking until a froth settles on top, then bring slowly to the boil. Remove from the heat and leave for 5 minutes.

4 Line a large strainer with a clean tea towel and place over a clean pan. Strain the soup into the pan, discarding the contents of the tea towel. Season the soup to taste, adding more sugar or lemon juice for a sweet-and-sour flavour. Set aside.

5 On a well-floured surface, roll out the piroshki dough to a 3 mm (¹/₈ inch) thickness, then cut out 6 cm (2¹/₂ inch) rounds using a plain cutter—you should have 8–12 rounds. Brush the edges of each round with a little beaten egg, and place a teaspoon of filling on one half of each. Fold the rounds over into turnovers, pinch the edges together to seal them, then leave the piroshki on a lightly floured tray for 10–15 minutes at room temperature.

6 Preheat a deep-fat fryer or deep pan, one-third full of oil, to 180°C (350°F). Cook the piroshki in batches until golden, then drain on crumpled paper towels and keep warm. Reheat the soup and transfer to warm bowls. Sprinkle with the snipped chives and serve the piroshki on the side.

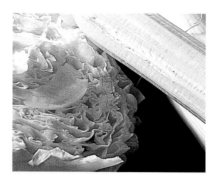

Pot-au-feu

Pot-au-feu literally means 'pot on the fire', and the long, slow cooking of this classic dish will fill your kitchen with sumptuous aromas as it gently simmers to perfection. The traditional vegetables used in this recipe could be changed to suit the season or your personal taste.

Preparation time **30 minutes**
Total cooking time **2 hours 45 minutes**
Serves **6–8**

2 small leeks
I celery stick or ¹/₂ small celeriac
8–10 black peppercorns
5–6 coriander seeds
¹/₂ small green or white cabbage, cut into quarters
250 g (8 oz) oxtail, cut into small pieces
750 g (1¹/₂ lb) beef ribs
I small veal knuckle
25 g (³/₄ oz) salt
I small onion, studded with 2 cloves
I clove garlic
bouquet garni (see page 63)
2 carrots, cut into 5 cm (2 inch) pieces
I turnip or swede, peeled and quartered

1 Tie the leek and celery or celeriac into a bundle. Place the peppercorns and coriander seeds in a small piece of muslin, tie up and set aside. Place the cabbage in a large pan and cover with cold water. Bring to the boil, cook for 3 minutes, then drain and rinse in cold water and set aside.

2 Rinse all the meat and bones, place them in a large pot and cover with cold water. Bring to the boil, then remove from the heat and drain. Rinse the meat again, return to the pot and cover with 3.5 litres cold water. Add the salt and bring to the boil. Skim off the foam and any fat that rises to the surface. Add the onion, garlic, bouquet garni and the sachet of peppercorns and coriander seeds. Simmer over low heat for at least 1 hour 45 minutes.

3 Add the carrot, turnip, cabbage and the leek and celery bundle. Cook for another 30 minutes, or until the meat is tender. Remove and discard the bouquet garni and the sachet of spices. Strain the meat and vegetables, reserving the bouillon. Arrange the meat on a large platter with the vegetables around, and serve the bouillon in a soup tureen.

Chef's tips This dish is traditionally served with cornichon pickles or cocktail gherkins, and salt for the meat.

Boiled potatoes may be added to the bouillon.

Trout flans with chive and lemon sauce

*These delicately flavoured and fine textured flans, served with a smooth lemon butter sauce,
make an elegant first course to impress your friends and dinner guests.*

Preparation time **30 minutes**
Total cooking time **30 minutes**
Serves 4

TROUT FLANS
fresh flat-leaf parsley leaves, to garnish
300 g (10 oz) skinned, trimmed and boned trout
1/4 teaspoon salt
pinch of cayenne pepper
I egg
150 ml (5 fl oz) thick (double) cream
200 ml (6 1/2 fl oz) milk

CHIVE AND LEMON SAUCE
I French shallot, finely chopped
juice of I lemon
**150 g (5 oz) unsalted butter, chilled and cut into
   small cubes**
I tablespoon very finely chopped fresh chives

1 Preheat the oven to warm 160°C (315°F/Gas 2–3).
Prepare four 8 x 4 cm (3 x 1 1/2 inch) ramekin moulds
by cutting four rounds of baking paper to the same
diameter. Grease the ramekins, then line them with the
rounds of baking paper and brush the lining with
softened butter, pressing out any air holes. Press one or
two parsley leaves onto the baking paper, then set aside
in the refrigerator.

2 To make the flan mixture, cut the trout into 1 cm
(1/2 inch) cubes and place in a food processor with the
salt, cayenne pepper and the egg. Blend until smooth.
Scrape down with a spatula and process again. With
the machine still running, add the cream and milk,
stopping the moment the liquid is incorporated—the
mixture should resemble a cake batter. Push the
mixture through a sieve into a jug.

3 Pour the mixture into the ramekins, tapping them on
a work surface to remove any air bubbles. Smooth the
tops and transfer the ramekins to a small roasting pan
lined with one or two sheets of paper towel, spacing
them evenly apart. Fill the pan with boiling water to
come halfway up the sides of the ramekins; transfer to
the oven and bake for 15–20 minutes. Insert a small knife
in the centre of a ramekin for 3 seconds. If the blade
comes out hot, the flans are cooked. Remove from the
hot water bath and set aside to rest. Keep warm.

4 To make the chive and lemon sauce, place the shallot
and lemon juice in a small saucepan. Add 2 tablespoons
water, bring to the boil and allow to reduce for about
5–7 minutes, or until almost dry. Reduce the heat to
low, then whisk in the butter, a few pieces at a time,
without letting the sauce boil. Strain into a clean pan
and season to taste with salt and freshly ground white
pepper. Just before serving, whisk in the chives.

5 Loosen the flans from the inside of the ramekins
using a small knife. Gently turn the flans out onto
individual serving plates. Carefully remove the paper,
drizzle the sauce around and serve immediately.

Chef's tip When making a lightly coloured sauce, use
ground white pepper rather than black pepper.

Scallops dieppoise

Dieppe, on the northern coast of France, is renowned for seafood specialities such as this. 'Dieppoise' dishes usually contain prawns, mussels, mushrooms and white wine.

Preparation time **1 hour**
Total cooking time **50 minutes**
Serves **4**

1 large French shallot, chopped
400 ml (12³/4 fl oz) white wine
2 sprigs of fresh thyme
1 bay leaf
250 g (8 oz) mussels, scrubbed and beards removed
250 g (8 oz) small raw prawns, shelled and deveined
20 scallops, shelled, dark vein removed
250 g (8 oz) button mushrooms, sliced
200 ml (6¹/2 fl oz) thick (double) cream
1 tablespoon chopped fresh flat-leaf parsley

1 Place the shallot, wine, thyme, bay leaf and mussels in a large pot. Bring to the boil, reduce the heat and simmer, covered, until the mussels open, tossing gently once or twice. Remove the mussels and allow to cool, discarding any that have not opened.
2 Line a fine sieve with a clean damp tea towel and strain the liquid into a large pan. Discard the contents of the tea towel, rinse it well, and set it up as before.
3 Bring the liquid to a simmer. Add the prawns, stir, then add the scallops. Cover and simmer for 5 minutes, or until the seafood is firm. Remove the seafood and set aside. Scoop the mussels from their shells and set aside.
4 Strain the cooking liquid through the tea towel into a saucepan. Bring to the boil, add the mushrooms and cook for about 25 minutes, or until almost dry. Add the cream and boil for 5 minutes. Add the seafood and simmer until hot. Season to taste and stir in the parsley just before serving.

Consommé with chicken quenelles

A consommé is a clarified meat or fish broth that should be crystal-clear and full of flavour.
Here it is served with light chicken quenelles and garnished with chervil.

Preparation time **30 minutes + chilling**
Total cooking time **2 hours 40 minutes**
Serves 4–6

1 chicken, weighing 1.75 kg (3¹/2 lb)
1 chicken Maryland (leg-quarter)
2–3 sets of giblets, minus the liver (optional)
1 large carrot
1 large onion, studded with a clove
1 celery stick
1 leek
1 ripe tomato
sprig of fresh thyme
5 fresh parsley stalks
1 bay leaf
6 black peppercorns
2 cloves garlic, crushed
¹/2 tablespoon brandy
sprigs of fresh chervil, to garnish

QUENELLES
1 egg white
75 ml (2¹/2 fl oz) thick (double) cream
small pinch of freshly grated nutmeg

FOR THE CLARIFICATION
1 small carrot, chopped
¹/2 celery stick, chopped
¹/2 leek, chopped
1 tomato, chopped
3 egg whites, lightly beaten

1 Remove the breast meat from the chicken, discarding the skin. Reserve and refrigerate for the quenelles. Bone the chicken leg-quarter, discarding all skin and fat. Chop the meat, cover and refrigerate for the clarification.

2 Place the remaining chicken meat and bones in a large pan with the giblets. Add enough cold water to cover and bring to the boil. Drain, rinse with cold water and return to the pan.

3 Add the whole vegetables, thyme, parsley, bay leaf, peppercorns and garlic, with 3.5 litres water and some salt. Bring to the boil, reduce the heat and simmer gently for 1¹/2–2 hours, skimming occasionally. Leave to cool, then remove the chicken and set aside. Strain the stock (there should be about 1.5 litres) into a clean pan, discarding the solids. Refrigerate, then skim off any fat.

4 To make the quenelles, purée the chicken breast in a food processor. Add the egg white, and process until smooth and superfine. Transfer to a bowl set in another bowl of iced water, then gradually beat in the cream. Season with salt, pepper and nutmeg.

5 Bring the stock to a simmer in a large pan. Test the chicken breast mixture for seasoning and shape into quenelles, following the Chef's techniques on page 62. Poach the quenelles in the simmering stock in batches for 5 minutes, or until just firm enough to remove with a slotted spoon. Place on a plate, cover and set aside.

6 Slightly overseason the stock. To clarify the stock, add the chicken leg meat, chopped carrot, celery, leek, tomato and egg whites. Mix well. Slowly bring to the boil, stirring until the egg whites solidify into a soft foamy crust. Reduce the heat to low and leave to simmer for 20–25 minutes.

7 Without pressing the solids, carefully strain the stock through a muslin-lined sieve into a clean pan; discard the solids. Reheat the consommé and add the brandy. Place the quenelles in bowls, ladle the consommé over and garnish with the chervil.

Country-style terrine

This coarsely-textured pâté derives its name from the deep rectangular dish in which it is cooked. Meat terrines often contain a high proportion of pork, and some pork fat, to prevent the meat from becoming dry.

Preparation time **30 minutes + 2 nights refrigeration**
Total cooking time **50 minutes**
Serves **6–8**

20 g (³/4 oz) unsalted butter
2 cloves garlic, chopped
2 French shallots, chopped
3 sprigs of fresh thyme
1 small bay leaf
200 g (6¹/2 oz) pork fat, finely diced
150 g (5 oz) calf, lamb or ox liver, finely diced
400 g (12³/4 oz) pork loin, finely diced
40 ml (1¹/4 fl oz) brandy
50 ml (1³/4 fl oz) white wine
¹/2 teaspoon salt
¹/4 teaspoon ground nutmeg
50 g (1³/4 oz) fresh breadcrumbs
1 tablespoon milk
1 egg, beaten
20 rashers streaky bacon, for lining

1 Melt the butter in a pan over low heat. Warm the garlic, shallots, thyme and bay leaf with the pork fat, liver and pork loin. Gently cook for 3–5 minutes. Add the brandy, wine, salt, nutmeg and some pepper, stirring well to coat the meat—the mixture should be warm, not hot. Leave to cool, then refrigerate overnight.

2 Preheat the oven to moderate 180°C (350°F/Gas 4). Wrap a small piece of wood or stiff cardboard (the same size as the top of a 1 litre terrine) in aluminium foil. Soak the breadcrumbs in milk.

3 Remove the thyme and bay leaf from the terrine mixture. Process the meat in a food processor in short bursts until roughly chopped, then transfer to a bowl. Mix together the breadcrumbs and egg and add to the meat. Mix well.

4 Line a greased terrine mould with bacon, letting the rashers hang over the sides. Add the meat mixture, fold the rashers over and cover with a layer of bacon, then a sheet of greased baking paper. Place in a baking pan half-filled with hot water and bake for 30–40 minutes. To check the temperature, insert the tip of a small knife into the centre of the terrine for a few seconds. If the blade comes out hot, the terrine is cooked; if not, cook for another 5 minutes, or until the knife comes out hot.

5 Remove from the oven and cool for 20 minutes. Place the wood or cardboard across the top, then weigh it down with a heavy can. Refrigerate overnight. Leave the terrine at room temperature for at least 30 minutes before serving. It can be served in the mould, or turned out onto a board or plate.

Beef Wellington

Beef Wellington is the name given to fillet of beef, lightly covered with duxelles (shallots and mushrooms cooked in butter) and/or a good liver pâté, then wrapped in puff pastry and cooked until golden.

Preparation time 1 hour + 15 minutes chilling
Total cooking time 1 hour 15 minutes
Serves 6

1.6 kg (3 lb 4 oz) beef eye fillet
120 ml (4 fl oz) oil
1 small carrot, chopped
1 small onion, chopped
1 small leek, chopped
50 ml (1³/4 fl oz) dry Madeira or sherry
500 ml (16 fl oz) brown stock (see page 63)
50 g (1³/4 oz) unsalted butter
2 French shallots, finely chopped
1 clove garlic, finely chopped
500 g (1 lb) button mushrooms, finely chopped
800 g (1 lb 10 oz) block puff pastry
10 slices Parma ham
1 egg, beaten

1 Preheat the oven to hot 220°C (425°F/Gas 7). Remove and reserve the thin muscle from the side of the main beef fillet. Remove and discard the shiny surface membrane and tie the fillet with string at 2 cm (³/4 inch) intervals.

2 Roughly chop the beef trimmings. Heat 1 tablespoon of the oil in a shallow pan, then add the beef trimmings and chopped carrot, onion and leek. Gently fry until the mixture browns. Stir in the Madeira, scraping up the sticky juices from the base of the pan, then simmer for a few minutes, or until reduced to a syrup. Stir in the stock. Bring to the boil, then reduce the heat and leave for 1 hour to simmer to a syrupy sauce while preparing the Beef Wellington.

3 Place an ovenproof pan over high heat and add the remaining oil. When a haze forms, add the beef fillet and brown quickly all over. Season well, then transfer to the oven and roast for about 5 minutes for medium rare, 10 minutes for medium and 15 minutes for well done. (The actual cooking time will depend on the thickness of the fillet.) Remove from the pan to cool completely.

4 Melt the butter in a saucepan and gently cook the shallots for 1–2 minutes, or until soft but not browned. Add the garlic and mushrooms and cook gently until the pan looks dry when scraped with a wooden spoon. The mixture should be barely moist. Set aside.

5 On a lightly floured work surface, roll the pastry 5 mm (¹/4 inch) thick, into a rectangle 35 x 60 cm (14 x 24 inches). Transfer to a baking tray, cover with plastic wrap and refrigerate for 15 minutes.

6 Transfer the pastry to the work surface. To reduce excess overlap, cut away each corner, reserving the pastry trimmings and leaving the centre large enough for the fillet—the pastry will resemble a cross. Flatten each flap of pastry with a rolling pin.

7 Lay the ham slices on the pastry and spread thinly with half the mushrooms. Untie the fillet, season well, place it on the pastry and spread with the remaining mushrooms. Bring the flaps of ham over the fillet. Brush the pastry edges with a little beaten egg and fold them over each other to completely envelop the fillet.

8 Turn onto a lightly buttered baking tray, seam-side-down. Cut the excess pastry into strips and crisscross a lattice pattern over the top. Brush with more beaten egg, then pierce a small slit in the top for a crisp finish. Place in the oven for 5 minutes to set, then lower the heat to moderately hot 200°C (400°F/Gas 6) and bake for 20 minutes.

9 Remove from the oven and rest for 10 minutes in a warm place. Skim any froth from the simmering sauce, then strain into a sauce boat. Slice the Beef Wellington and serve at once.

Lamb medallions with redcurrant sauce

This superb dish, with its classic combination of redcurrant and lamb, may seem very time consuming.
Rest assured, it isn't: most of the cooking time revolves around a gently simmering pot.

*Preparation time **45 minutes + overnight marinating***
*Total cooking time **2 hours 10 minutes***
Serves 4

3 x 8-chop racks of lamb (best end of neck) or
  I saddle of lamb (ask your butcher to debone the
  lamb, remove the fat, chop the bones and reserve
  the trimmings)
oil, for cooking
I tablespoon tomato paste
I tablespoon sugar
I tablespoon red wine vinegar
I teaspoon crushed black pepper
2 tablespoons redcurrant jelly
250 ml (8 fl oz) brown stock (see page 63)

MARINADE
I carrot, diced
I onion, diced
I celery stick, diced
I French shallot, diced
2 tomatoes, diced
4 juniper berries
4 cloves garlic, split in half
I tablespoon red wine vinegar
I tablespoon oil
bouquet garni (see page 63)
1.5 litres heavy red wine

1 Place the lamb bones and trimmings in a large bowl with all the marinade ingredients except the wine. Bring the wine to the boil in a pan, then pour directly into the marinade bowl. Leave to cool, then add the lamb fillets and marinate overnight, or for a maximum of 48 hours.

2 Remove the fillets from the marinade. Pat dry, cover with plastic wrap and refrigerate until ready to use. Strain the marinade into a pan, reserving the bones and vegetables. Bring to the boil, then reduce the heat and leave to simmer gently while browning the bones.

3 Heat about 2 tablespoons of oil in a large pan. Brown the bones over medium heat for 10–15 minutes, or until dry and well coloured, stirring constantly to prevent burning. Drain the pan of excess oil and return the bones to the pan. Add the vegetables and cook for 2–3 minutes, or until lightly coloured. Mix in the tomato paste and cook for 1 minute.

4 Strain the hot marinade into the pan and bring to the boil, scraping the base of the pan to dissolve the cooking juices. Add enough water to cover the bones completely, then reduce the heat and simmer for 1 hour, skimming regularly. Strain the sauce through a fine sieve and discard the bones and vegetables. Cook for about 20 minutes, or until reduced in volume to 250 ml (8 fl oz), skimming regularly.

5 In a heavy-based saucepan, melt the sugar over medium heat for 2–3 minutes, or until caramelised. Remove from the heat and immediately add the vinegar, taking care not to breathe in the fumes. Mix until the caramel dissolves, then add the pepper, half the redcurrant jelly, the stock and reduced marinade. Simmer for 5 minutes, then strain through a fine sieve, into a clean pan. Cook for a further 5 minutes, or until the sauce is thick enough to coat the back of a spoon. Stir in the rest of the redcurrant jelly. Season with salt and keep warm.

6 Cut the fillets into 16 medallions, each about 2.5 cm (1 inch) thick. Heat 2 tablespoons of oil in a frying pan over medium-high heat. Season the medallions with salt and freshly ground pepper, then cook for 2–3 minutes on each side. Serve with the hot sauce.

Pork chops with sage

Sage, a wonderfully redolent herb, marries perfectly with the tang of mustard in this delectable dish.

Preparation time **15 minutes**
Total cooking time **45 minutes**
Serves 4

4 pork chops cut from the rib, about 180 g
 (5³/4 oz) each
8 fresh sage leaves
30 g (1 oz) unsalted butter
oil, for cooking
2 French shallots, finely chopped
2 teaspoons light-coloured honey
juice of ¹/2 lemon
200 ml (6¹/2 fl oz) white wine
350 ml (11¹/4 fl oz) brown stock (see page 63)
2 tablespoons Dijon mustard

1　Preheat the oven to moderate 180°C (350°F/Gas 4). Trim the pork chops well and season with salt and pepper. Set aside the four nicest sage leaves to garnish, and finely shred the others.

2　Heat the butter and a tablespoon of oil in an ovenproof frying pan. Brown the chops on both sides over medium heat, then transfer to the oven and roast for 15 minutes.

3　Once cooked, remove the chops from the pan; cover and keep warm. Add the shallots to the pan and cook over medium heat, without colouring, for 2–3 minutes, then add the honey and lemon juice and cook until the mixture is syrupy.

4　Add the wine, scraping the bottom of the pan well. Add the stock and simmer for 10–15 minutes, or until reduced in volume by half. Whisk in the mustard, being careful not to let the sauce boil.

5　Strain the sauce, mix in the shredded sage, and adjust the seasoning. Coat the warm chops with the sauce, garnish each with a sage leaf and serve immediately.

Roasted duck with turnips

Roasting a duck on each side before turning it onto its back will ensure the breast fillets do not dry out. The salty bacon and sweetened turnips perfectly complement this succulent dish.

Preparation time **40 minutes**
Total cooking time **1 hour 40 minutes**
Serves 4

1.4 kg (2 lb 13 oz) duck, trussed (ask your butcher to do this)
oil, for cooking
60 g (2 oz) unsalted butter, softened
200 g (6 1/2 oz) duck trimmings (wings or necks), chopped
1 kg (2 lb) turnips
300 g (10 oz) bacon, cut into 1 cm (1/2 inch) cubes
20 g (3/4 oz) unsalted butter
1 teaspoon sugar
1 French shallot, chopped
1 tablespoon chopped celery
1 tablespoon chopped carrot
1 tablespoon chopped onion
750 ml (24 fl oz) chicken stock (see page 62)
bouquet garni (see page 63)

1 Preheat the oven to moderately hot 200°C (400°F/ Gas 6). Coat a roasting pan with 2 tablespoons of oil. Season the duck, rub it all over with oil and place it on its side in the pan. Dot with the softened butter, transfer to the oven and roast for 20 minutes, basting every 5 minutes. Turn the duck onto its other side and roast for 20 more minutes, basting as before. Turn the duck on its back, add the duck trimmings, then roast and baste for another 15 minutes.

2 Peel the turnips and use a melon-baller to scoop the flesh into little balls. Place the balls in cold water until ready to use.

3 In a frying pan, heat some oil and brown the bacon over medium heat. Strain and set aside. Drain and dry the turnips; place in the pan with the butter, sugar and some salt. Cover with cold water and cook over high heat until evaporated. Roll the turnips until coated and shiny. Remove from the heat, add the bacon and set aside.

4 Remove the duck from the roasting pan; cover and keep warm. Remove and drain the trimmings. Drain the pan of all but 2 tablespoons of the oil and duck juices and place over low heat for 10 minutes, or until the juices are sticky and the fat is clear.

5 Add the trimmings and chopped vegetables and cook for 2 minutes. Add the stock and bouquet garni; stir well and pour into a pan. Bring to the boil, reduce the heat and simmer, skimming occasionally, for 20–30 minutes, or until the sauce is reduced by half. Strain, discarding the solids; season and keep warm.

6 Remove the string and place the duck on a platter. Reheat the bacon and turnips and arrange around the duck. Drizzle half the sauce over the bacon and turnips and serve the remaining sauce on the side.

Chef's tip For instructions on carving the duck, refer to the Chef's techniques on page 63.

Blanquette of lamb in garlic cream

*'Blanquette de veau', a very traditional French stew, has here been updated into a modern
classic, using lamb in place of the veal and flavoured heartily with garlic.*

Preparation time **20 minutes**
Total cooking time **1 hour 40 minutes**
Serves 6

1 lamb shoulder, about 1.5 kg (3 lb), deboned
1 carrot
1 small onion
1 celery stick
1 sprig of fresh thyme or 1/2 teaspoon dried thyme
bay leaf
1 teaspoon salt
10–12 peppercorns
8 unpeeled cloves garlic
100 ml (3 1/4 fl oz) olive oil
30 g (1 oz) unsalted butter
30 g (1 oz) plain flour
300 ml (10 fl oz) cream
finely chopped fresh parsley, to garnish

1 Trim the lamb of excess fat and cut the meat into
3 cm (1 1/4 inch) cubes. Place the lamb cubes in a large
flameproof casserole dish with the whole carrot, onion,
celery stick, the thyme, bay leaf, salt and peppercorns.
Add cold water to reach 2.5 cm (1 inch) above the meat
and vegetables. Bring to the boil, then reduce the heat
and simmer for about 1 hour 10 minutes, skimming any
froth from the surface.

2 Meanwhile, set the oven to its lowest temperature.
Place the garlic cloves in a small ovenproof dish and
cover with the olive oil. Cook for 40 minutes, or until
soft. Drain and peel the garlic cloves, then press through
a sieve to obtain a purée.

3 Strain and reserve the liquid. Discard the vegetables
and keep the lamb warm. Return the liquid to the
casserole and simmer over low heat for 20 minutes, or
until reduced by half, skimming off the excess fat.

4 Melt the butter in a saucepan over low heat. Add the
flour and cook for 1 minute. Add the reduced cooking
liquid and whisk to the boil. Add the cream and mix
until smooth, then add the garlic purée. Strain the sauce
and season to taste with salt and freshly ground pepper.
Arrange the lamb in a deep serving dish and cover with
the sauce. Sprinkle with the parsley and serve at once.

Roast beef and Yorkshire puddings

What could be more tantalising and traditional than roast beef served with crisp, golden Yorkshire puddings and lightly tangy horseradish cream? Carve the beef at the table for the greatest effect.

Preparation time **40 minutes + 30 minutes resting**
Total cooking time **1 hour 40 minutes**
Serves 4–6

YORKSHIRE PUDDINGS
175 ml (5³/4 fl oz) milk
175 g (5³/4 oz) plain flour
2 eggs

oil, for cooking
1.5 kg (3 lb) sirloin of beef, rolled and tied

HORSERADISH CREAM
120 ml (4 fl oz) cream, for whipping
40 g (1¹/4 oz) grated fresh horseradish
a few drops of lemon juice

JUS
1 carrot, chopped
1 onion, chopped
1 celery stick, chopped
1 leek, chopped
1 bay leaf
2 sprigs of fresh thyme
3 peppercorns
500 ml (16 fl oz) brown stock (see page 63)

1 Preheat the oven to hot 220°C (425°F/Gas 7). To make the Yorkshire puddings, combine the milk with 125 ml (4 fl oz) water. Sift the flour and some salt into a bowl and make a well in the centre. Add the eggs and begin to whisk. As the mixture thickens, gradually add the milk and water, whisking until a smooth batter forms. Pour into a jug, cover and stand for 30 minutes.
2 On the stove top, heat about 3 tablespoons of oil in a roasting pan over high heat. Add the beef sirloin, fat-side-down, and brown all over, turning with tongs. Transfer the beef to the oven and, turning and basting every 15 minutes, roast for 30 minutes for rare, 45 minutes for medium-rare, and 1 hour for well done.
3 To make the horseradish cream, lightly whip the cream until soft peaks form. Gently fold in the grated horseradish and season to taste with salt, freshly ground pepper and the lemon juice. Do not overfold or the mixture will become too thick. Transfer to a serving bowl, cover and chill.
4 Transfer the beef to a plate, cover lightly with foil and allow to rest for 10–15 minutes before carving. Leaving a tablespoon of fat in the roasting pan, drain the excess fat and use it to brush a deep, 12-hole patty tin.
5 Heat the patty tray in the oven for 2–3 minutes until lightly smoking. Fill each patty hole with the Yorkshire pudding batter and bake for 15–20 minutes, or until puffed and golden.
6 To make the jus, heat the remaining fat in the roasting pan over the stove top. Add the vegetables and gently fry over medium heat for 5 minutes, or until golden, stirring constantly. Drain the pan of any excess fat; add the bay leaf, thyme, peppercorns and a little hot stock, scraping the base of the pan with a wooden spoon. Add the remaining hot stock and simmer to reduce by half, skimming off any foam or fat. Strain into a saucepan, discarding the vegetables and seasonings. Skim again, season to taste, then cover and keep warm. (Pour into a warm sauce boat just before serving.)
7 Serve the beef and puddings on warm plates, with the jus and horseradish cream on the side. Green vegetables and roast potatoes are traditional accompaniments.

Chef's tip Resting a roast makes the meat easier to carve and helps prevent the juices running. Any juices from the resting can be poured over the meat, but do not add them to the jus: they will spoil its texture.

Salmon, leek and potato gratin

This wonderful recipe, combining fresh and smoked salmon, is perfect for a special lunch or supper.
A more economical version, also delicious, could be made using any fresh fish, or even salt cod.

*Preparation time **20 minutes***
*Total cooking time **50 minutes***
Serves 6

800 g (1 lb 10 oz) floury potatoes
220 g (7 oz) unsalted butter, softened
3 small leeks, thinly sliced
150 g (5 oz) salmon fillet, skinned
200 g (6¹/₂ oz) smoked salmon, diced
300 ml (10 fl oz) cream
100 g (3¹/₄ oz) grated Swiss cheese
40 g (1¹/₄ oz) unsalted butter, chopped
sprigs of fresh dill, to garnish

1 Peel the potatoes and place in a large pan of salted water. Bring to the boil, then reduce the heat and simmer for 20–25 minutes, or until tender to the point of a knife. Drain and finely mash the potatoes, or purée them using a food mill or ricer. Mix in half the softened butter and keep warm.

2 Melt the remaining softened butter in a frying pan over low heat. Gently cook the leeks for 2–3 minutes, without colouring. Drain the excess butter and spread the leeks evenly in an oval gratin dish. Set aside.

3 Remove any fine bones from the fresh salmon using a pair of tweezers. Place the fillet in a steamer basket, then cover and steam for 5–10 minutes, or until the fish changes colour and begins to break apart when pressed with a fork. Break the fish into pieces and mix into the mashed potato with the smoked salmon.

4 Preheat the grill to hot. Bring the cream to the boil in a pan, then stir into the salmon and potato mixture. Mix well and season to taste. Transfer to the gratin dish and sprinkle with the grated cheese. Dot with the butter and brown under the grill for 2–3 minutes, or until golden. Serve garnished with sprigs of dill.

Chef's tip To use salt cod in this recipe, rinse and soak it overnight, then poach in milk with a few sprigs of fresh thyme, a bay leaf and a few garlic cloves until tender. Drain, break into small pieces, then add to the potato mixture.

Normandy pork

Normandy lies along France's northern Atlantic coastline and is famous for its dairy farming and apple production. Not surprisingly, the cuisine of this region often features apples, cream, cider or Calvados—or sometimes all four, as in this superb dish.

Preparation time **25 minutes**
Total cooking time **55 minutes**
Serves 4

2 small apples, such as Golden Delicious
juice of 1/2 lemon
80 g (2³/4 oz) unsalted butter
600 g (1 1/4 lb) pork fillets
oil, for cooking
1 onion, chopped
1 carrot, chopped
sprig of fresh thyme
1 bay leaf
350 ml (11 1/4 fl oz) dry cider
20 ml (³/4 fl oz) Calvados or apple brandy
375 ml (12 fl oz) thick (double) cream

1 Peel and core the apples, reserving the cores and peelings. Cut the apples into 1 cm (1/2 inch) cubes (keep all the trimmings) and toss them in the lemon juice. In a non-stick frying pan, melt half the butter and cook the apples over medium heat for 5 minutes, or until golden brown. Drain and transfer to a plate, spreading out the apples to help them cool quickly.

2 Trim the fat and sinew from the pork fillets, reserving the trimmings. Cut the pork into thick medallions and season well.

3 Heat the remaining butter and a tablespoon of oil in a heavy-based frying pan. Cook the pork medallions over medium heat for 8 minutes on each side, or until nicely coloured. Remove from the pan, cover with aluminium foil, set aside and keep warm.

4 Add the pork trimmings to the pan and brown for 5–7 minutes, or until golden. Drain the pan of excess oil, then add the apple trimmings, onion, carrot, thyme and bay leaf. Cook over medium heat for 5–7 minutes.

5 Add the cider and Calvados and cook for 5 minutes, or until reduced in volume by half. Add the cream, reduce the heat and simmer for 10 minutes. Strain the sauce, discard the solids and simmer for 1 minute more before adding the diced cooked apple. Cook for another 2 minutes, then season to taste. Keep hot.

6 Transfer the pork medallions to a frying pan. Pour the sauce over them and simmer for 2–3 minutes, or until heated through.

Roasted lamb with vegetables

This memorable roast is served with a classic French garnish of bacon, mushrooms, glazed pearl onions and golden brown potatoes. It makes a special dish for a Sunday lunch with all the family.

Preparation time 1 hour 15 minutes
Total cooking time 1 hour
Serves 6

100 ml (3¹/4 fl oz) oil
1 lamb shoulder, about 1.5 kg (3 lb), deboned
 (ask your butcher to tie the lamb, chop the bones
 and reserve the trimmings)
1 carrot, chopped
1 onion, chopped
¹/2 celery stick, chopped
2 cloves garlic, crushed
1 sprig of fresh thyme or ¹/4 teaspoon dried thyme
1 bay leaf
300 g (10 oz) bacon
300 g (10 oz) pearl onions or large-bulb spring onions,
 peeled
70 g (2¹/4 oz) unsalted butter
1 tablespoon sugar
300 g (10 oz) button mushrooms
1 kg (2 lb) potatoes, peeled
375 ml (12 fl oz) chicken stock (see page 62)
2 tablespoons chopped fresh parsley

1 Preheat the oven to moderately hot 200°C (400°F/ Gas 6). Heat half the oil in a large ovenproof frying pan over high heat. Season the lamb and brown on all sides in the hot oil. Remove and set aside. Add the bones and trimmings to the pan and brown all over.

2 Add the carrot, onion, celery, garlic, thyme and bay leaf to the pan. Rest the lamb on the bones, then transfer to the oven and roast for 40 minutes for rare, or 1 hour for medium, basting two or three times.

3 Cut the bacon into 3 mm (¹/8 inch) pieces. In a pan, lightly brown the bacon, then drain. Place the pearl onions in a medium saucepan over high heat with a tablespoon of the butter, the sugar, 50 ml (1³/4 fl oz) water, and salt and freshly ground pepper to taste. Cook until the water has evaporated and the onions are a light blond colour.

4 Cut the mushrooms into quarters, then sauté them in a tablespoon of the butter over high heat until browned. Season to taste and drain.

5 Using a melon-baller, carve the potatoes into balls, placing them in cold water to prevent browning, then transfer to a pan of cold water. Bring to the boil, boil for 1 minute, then drain.

6 Heat the remaining oil in an ovenproof pan over high heat. When the oil is hot, add the potatoes, tossing to coat them evenly with oil. Cook for 2–3 minutes, or until well coloured, then transfer to the oven and bake for 20 minutes, or until tender. Drain off the excess oil, toss the potato balls in a tablespoon of the butter and season to taste.

7 Remove the lamb from the oven and place on a wire rack to rest. Drain the pan of excess fat, remove the bones and trimmings, and place the pan on the stove top over medium-high heat. Cook for 2–3 minutes, or until the vegetables have coloured, then add the stock and stir to dissolve the cooking juices. Cook for about 10 minutes, or until reduced in volume by a third. Strain through a sieve and season to taste.

8 Toss together the pearl onions, potatoes, mushrooms and bacon and reheat if necessary. Sprinkle with the chopped parsley. Carve the lamb into slices about 1 cm (¹/2 inch) thick; serve with the vegetables and bacon arranged around, and the sauce on the side.

Steak and kidney pudding

Originally from Sussex, this famous English dish features morsels of steak and kidney in a thick, rich gravy, enclosed in suet pastry. It can be enriched with the addition of mushrooms, or even oysters.

*Preparation time **50 minutes***
*Total cooking time **4 hours***
*Serves **6***

2 tablespoons plain flour
500 g (1 lb) blade or chuck steak, cut into 1 cm
*   (1/2 inch) cubes*
200 g (6 1/2 oz) ox or calf kidney, core removed,
*   cut into 5 mm (1/4 inch) pieces*
50–75 g (1 3/4– 2 1/2 oz) button mushrooms, quartered
2 small onions, finely chopped
2 tablespoons chopped fresh parsley
1 tablespoon Worcestershire sauce
60–125 ml (2–4 fl oz) brown stock (see page 63)

SUET PASTRY
350 g (11 1/4 oz) self-raising flour
175 g (5 3/4 oz) beef suet, grated

1 Grease a 1.5 litre pudding basin. Place the flour in a large bowl, season with salt and pepper, then toss with the steak and kidney. Add the mushrooms, onion, parsley and Worcestershire sauce. Mix lightly, season, and set aside. Place an upturned saucer or trivet in a large pan, fill to a third with water and bring to the boil.

2 To make the suet pastry, sift the flour and some salt into a bowl. Toss in the suet and make a well in the centre. Mix lightly using a round-bladed knife, then gradually add just enough water to obtain a reasonably stiff paste.

3 On a well floured surface, roll out two thirds of the pastry to fit the basin. Carefully ease the pastry into the basin, checking there are no creases, and extending the pastry over the edges of the bowl. Roll out the remaining pastry to a circle 1.5 cm (5/8 inch) thick and the same size as the top of the pudding basin. Set aside as a lid. Fill the pastry-lined basin with the meat, adding enough stock to cover the meat. Turn the excess pastry over the filling and moisten lightly, then press the pastry lid on lightly to seal.

4 Cover with greaseproof paper, then aluminium foil, turning the edges under. Cover with a pudding cloth or tea towel and tie some kitchen string securely under the rim to keep it in place. As a handle, tie a knot over the pudding with the cloth ends. Place on the saucer in the pan of simmering water and steam for 4 hours, adding boiling water as needed so the pan does not boil dry.

5 Remove the cloth, foil and paper and clean the outside of the basin. Wrap a clean napkin around and serve the pudding from the basin, or turn the pudding out onto a plate for slicing and serving.

Stuffed veal escalopes

*These impressive veal parcels enclosing a meat, ham and mushroom filling are served here with
a hearty tomato sauce flavoured with Armagnac, a French brandy from Gascony.*

*Preparation time **1 hour***
*Total cooking time **1 hour 15 minutes***
Serves 4

8 small veal escalopes, about 60 g (2 oz) each
16 rashers bacon, rind removed
plain flour, for dusting

FILLING
100 g (3¼ oz) minced veal
100 g (3¼ oz) minced pork loin
20 g (¾ oz) unsalted butter
2 French shallots, finely chopped
100 g (3¼ oz) mushrooms, chopped
30 g (1 oz) ham, chopped
1 tablespoon thick (double) cream
1½ tablespoons fresh breadcrumbs
30 ml (1 fl oz) Armagnac

ARMAGNAC SAUCE
30 g (1 oz) unsalted butter
1 small carrot, chopped
1 small onion, chopped
1 celery stick, chopped
50 ml (1¾ fl oz) Armagnac
1 tablespoon tomato paste
40 g (1¼ oz) plain flour
**500 ml (16 fl oz) chicken or brown stock (see
    pages 62 and 63)**
3 tomatoes, peeled, seeded and chopped
bouquet garni (see page 63)
2 cloves garlic, chopped

1 Preheat the oven to moderately hot 200°C (400°F/
Gas 6). Trim the veal of fat and sinew, reserving the
trimmings. Place the veal between two sheets of plastic
wrap and flatten with a meat mallet.

2 To make the filling, mix the minced meats in a bowl.
Melt the butter in a heavy-based pan. Add the shallots,
then the mushrooms, and cook over medium heat for
2–3 minutes, or until dry. Add the ham and cook for
2 minutes. Add the cream and simmer for 5 minutes, or
until thick. Remove from the heat and leave to cool,
then mix into the meat. Stir in the breadcrumbs and
Armagnac and season to taste.

3 Spread a thin layer of filling onto the veal, then roll
up into neat parcels. Wrap a bacon strip or two around
each one, then tie up with kitchen string like a package.

4 To make the Armagnac sauce, melt the butter in a
large flameproof casserole dish over medium heat.
Add the chopped carrot, onion, celery and veal trimmings,
and cook, without colouring, until the onions are
translucent. Add the Armagnac, cook for 2 minutes,
then add the tomato paste and cook for 1–2 minutes.
Sprinkle with the flour and cook for 2 minutes more.
Stir in the stock, tomatoes, bouquet garni and garlic.
Season to taste with salt and freshly ground pepper and
simmer for 10 minutes, skimming if necessary.

5 Melt some butter and oil in a frying pan over
medium heat. Lightly dust the veal escalopes with flour,
then brown them in the hot pan for 1–2 minutes. Add
them to the sauce, transfer to the oven and cook,
uncovered, for 25–30 minutes, basting once or twice.

6 Transfer the escalopes to a dish; set aside and keep
warm. Strain the sauce into a clean pan and cook for
10 minutes, skimming constantly. Remove and discard
the string and bacon from the escalopes and simmer the
parcels in the sauce for 1–2 minutes. Slice and serve
on individual plates with the sauce poured over,
surrounded by vegetables such as glazed carrots, and
onions sprinkled with chopped fresh parsley.

Lamb stew with potatoes

This homely stew is perfect fare to combat the chill of wintry evenings.

*Preparation time **45 minutes***
*Total cooking time **2 hours***
Serves 4

1 kg (2 lb) lamb shoulder, deboned
2 tablespoons oil
40 g (1 1/4 oz) unsalted butter
1 large onion, finely chopped
3 tablespoons tomato paste
1 tablespoon plain flour
2 large tomatoes, peeled, seeded and chopped
3 cloves garlic, chopped
1.5 litres chicken stock (see page 62)
bouquet garni (see page 63)
12 small potatoes
3 tablespoons chopped fresh parsley

1 Preheat the oven to moderately hot 200°C (400°F/ Gas 6). Trim the lamb of fat and sinew and cut the meat into 2.5 cm (1 inch) cubes. Heat the oil in a heavy-based frying pan, then brown the lamb over medium-high heat. Drain, cover and set aside.

2 In a flameproof casserole dish, melt the butter and cook the onion over medium heat for 5 minutes, then add the tomato paste and cook for 2 minutes. Stir in the flour and cook for 2 minutes more. Add the tomatoes and cook for 3 minutes, then add the garlic and mix well. Add the lamb and any juices.

3 In a separate pot, bring the stock to the boil, then add to the casserole and simmer for 1–2 minutes, skimming the foam. Add the bouquet garni and season to taste. Bake, covered, for 30 minutes. Uncover and bake for 30 minutes more.

4 Add the potatoes. Cook for another 20–30 minutes, or until the potatoes are tender. Remove the bouquet garni and stir in the parsley just before serving.

Treacle and almond tart

Served warm with some whipped cream or a little freshly made vanilla custard, this deliciously sweet tart will enrich any winter's meal.

Preparation time **30 minutes + 20 minutes refrigeration**
Total cooking time **35 minutes**
Serves 8

PASTRY
200 g (6¹/₂ oz) plain flour
large pinch of caster sugar
100 g (3¹/₄ oz) unsalted butter, chilled and cut into cubes
1 egg, lightly beaten
drop of vanilla extract or essence

FILLING
75 g (2¹/₂ oz) unsalted butter, melted
juice and finely grated rind of 1 lemon
100 g (3¹/₄ oz) golden syrup
100 g (3¹/₄ oz) treacle
180 g (5³/₄ oz) ground almonds
100 g (3¹/₄ oz) fresh breadcrumbs
1 egg, beaten
60 g (2 oz) flaked almonds, to decorate

1 Brush a 22 x 2.5 cm (9 x 1 inch) loose-bottomed flan tin with melted butter. To make the pastry, sift the flour, caster sugar and a large pinch of salt into a large bowl. Rub the cubes of cold butter into the flour with a fast flicking action of the thumbs across the fingertips, until the mixture resembles fine breadcrumbs.

2 Make a well in the centre and pour in the beaten egg, a teaspoon of water and a drop of vanilla. Slowly work the pastry together by hand, or stir with a round-bladed knife into a rough ball. If the pastry is slightly sticky, add a little more flour. Turn out onto a cool, lightly floured surface, and knead very gently for no more than 20 seconds so that the pastry is just smooth. Cover with plastic wrap and refrigerate for at least 20 minutes before using. Preheat the oven to moderately hot 200°C (400°F/Gas 6).

3 Roll the pastry on a floured surface to about 3 mm (¹/₈ inch) in thickness. Line the flan tin with the pastry, pushing the pastry into the flutes of the tin with the help of a small ball of excess pastry. Trim off the excess pastry using a sharp knife, or roll a rolling pin across the top of the tin. Cut a circle of baking paper 3 cm (1¹/₄ inches) larger than the flan tin, crush it into a ball, open it up and place it inside the pastry so that the sheet comes up the sides.

4 Fill the flan right up to the rim with rice or baking beans, then press down gently so they rest firmly against the sides of the flan. Transfer to the oven and bake for 12–15 minutes. Remove the rice or baking beans and discard the paper. If the pastry base looks wet, return the flan to the oven for 3–4 minutes. When cooked, remove from the oven and cool in the tin. Reduce the oven temperature to moderate 180°C (350°F/Gas 4).

5 To make the filling, combine all the filling ingredients except the flaked almonds in a large bowl. Stir briskly until smooth. Spread into the pastry case and sprinkle with the flaked almonds. Bake for 15 minutes, or until the mixture feels set to the light touch of a finger. Remove from the oven, leave in the flan tin and place on a wire rack to cool before serving.

Chef's tip For a lighter flavour, leave out the treacle and use another 100 g (3¹/₄ oz) of golden syrup instead.

Rhubarb and ginger pudding with caramel sauce

The sweetness of brown sugar and treacle in this comforting winter pudding is perfectly balanced by the tartness of rhubarb. The quantities of glacé ginger can be adjusted to taste.

*Preparation time **20 minutes***
*Total cooking time **1 hour***
Serves 8

4 eggs
100 g (3¹/4 oz) dark brown sugar
1 teaspoon treacle
100 g (3¹/4 oz) plain flour
1 teaspoon finely chopped glacé ginger
300 g (10 oz) rhubarb, trimmed and diced

CARAMEL SAUCE
200 ml (6¹/2 fl oz) thick (double) cream
150 g (5 oz) dark brown sugar
50 g (1³/4 oz) unsalted butter
1 teaspoon treacle (optional)
1 piece of glacé ginger, chopped (optional)

1 Preheat the oven to warm 170°C (325°F/Gas 3). Grease a round 20 x 6 cm (8 x 2¹/2 inch) cake tin and line the base with a circle of baking paper. Half-fill a pan with water, bring to the boil, then remove the pan from the heat.

2 Break the eggs into a heatproof bowl, add the brown sugar and place over the steaming pan of water, ensuring the bowl does not touch the water. Whisk until the mixture is thick and mousse-like, then remove the bowl from the water and whisk until cold. Whisk in the treacle until well blended. Sift the flour and gently fold into the mixture, ensuring all the flour is well incorporated to prevent lumps forming. Add the ginger.

3 Sprinkle half the diced rhubarb into the cake tin and cover with the pudding mixture. Sprinkle the remaining rhubarb over the top. Transfer to the oven and bake for 35–40 minutes, or until the pudding is firm to the touch and a skewer inserted into the centre comes out clean.

4 To make the caramel sauce, warm the cream in a small saucepan over low heat to prevent the caramel forming lumps when the cream is added. Place the brown sugar in a separate pan over high heat, stirring constantly. As the sugar starts to melt, remove the pan from the heat and slowly stir in the cream to warm through. Whisk in the butter, then add the treacle and ginger if desired. Keep warm.

5 Turn the pudding onto a plate; remove the tin and paper. Invert again and serve with the sauce drizzled around, with a scoop of vanilla ice cream if desired.

Chef's tip This pudding can be frozen. It can also be reheated in the microwave, covered with plastic wrap.

Fruit tarts with vanilla syrup

The autumnal colours of dried fruit turn these melt-in-the-mouth shortbread treats—known to the French as 'sablés aux fruits secs'—into an eye-catching delight.

*Preparation time **20 minutes + 30 minutes resting***
*Total cooking time **20 minutes***
Serves 4

SHORTBREAD PASTRY
250 g (8 oz) plain flour
60 g (2 oz) icing sugar
I teaspoon vanilla sugar (see Chef's tip)
170 g (5¹/2 oz) unsalted butter, chilled and
*   cut into cubes*

FRUIT TOPPING
280 g (9 oz) sugar
I vanilla pod, split in half
8 prunes, pitted
8 dried apricots
8 dates, pitted
I tablespoon currants
I carrot, very thinly sliced
I tablespoon chopped pistachios
I tablespoon sesame seeds
I tablespoon slivered almonds

1 Preheat the oven to moderate 180°C (350°F/Gas 4). To make the pastry, sift the dry ingredients and some salt onto a work surface. Make a well in the centre, add the butter and work in with the fingertips until a dough forms that can be shaped into a ball. Flatten gently, place between two sheets of greaseproof or baking paper, and roll out to a 5 mm (¹/4 inch) thickness. Transfer to a baking tray and chill for at least 20 minutes.

2 To make the fruit topping, place the sugar, vanilla pod and 265 ml (8¹/2 fl oz) water in a saucepan and bring to the boil. Remove from the heat and add the prunes, apricots, dates, currants and carrot. Cover and leave to soak for 10 minutes. Remove the vanilla pod. Reserving the liquid, thoroughly drain the fruit and set aside. Bring the liquid to the boil and cook over high heat for 5–10 minutes, or until reduced to a syrup.

3 Remove the top sheet of paper from the pastry and using a fluted cutter, cut four rounds 10 cm (4 inches) in diameter, placing them on a greased baking tray. Bake for 10 minutes, or until just golden.

4 Arrange the fruit among the four shortbread rounds. Sprinkle with the pistachios, sesame seeds and slivered almonds, and drizzle the syrup onto the serving plate around each shortbread. Serve with mascarpone or thick cream.

Chef's tip To make vanilla sugar, simply keep a vanilla pod in a jar of caster sugar.

Steamed orange pudding

Hot, light and full of flavour, this pudding will brighten the gloom of a winter's day like a burst of summer sunshine. Serve with orange sauce or custard.

*Preparation time **30 minutes***
*Total cooking time **1 hour 45 minutes***
Serves 6

100 g (3¹/4 oz) thin-cut marmalade
2 large oranges, peel and pith removed
125 g (4 oz) unsalted butter, at room temperature
125 g (4 oz) caster sugar
finely grated rind of 1 orange
2 large eggs, beaten
185 g (6 oz) self-raising flour
milk, for mixing

ORANGE SAUCE
320 ml (10¹/4 fl oz) orange juice
2 egg yolks
¹/2 teaspoon cornflour
45 g (1¹/2 oz) caster sugar
1 teaspoon Grand Marnier or Cointreau

1 Butter a 1.25 litre pudding basin measuring 15 cm (6 inches) across the top. Cut two 28 cm (11 inch) circles, one from greaseproof paper, one from foil. Place the paper on the foil, then brush the paper with softened butter. Fold the paper and foil to make a 2 cm (3/4 inch) pleat in the centre, to allow the pudding to expand.

2 Spoon the marmalade into the pudding basin. Finely slice the oranges, then line the basin with the orange slices, from the marmalade base to the top of the bowl.

3 In a bowl, beat the butter with a wooden spoon or electric whisk to soften. Slowly add the sugar, beating until light and fluffy. Mix in the orange rind. Add the egg in four additions, beating well between each

addition. Sift in the flour and quickly fold into the mixture using a large metal spoon or plastic spatula. As the last traces of flour are mixed in, add a little milk to form a soft consistency: the mixture should drop from the spoon with a flick of the wrist.

4 Immediately transfer the mixture to the pudding basin. Cover with the circle of paper and foil, placing the sheet foil-side-up, and tie with kitchen string to seal. Place a saucer or trivet in a large pan and rest the pudding basin upon it. Half-fill the pan with boiling water and bring to the boil. Ensuring the water is gently bubbling at all times, and topping up with boiling water as necessary, steam the pudding for 1¹/2–1³/4 hours, or until springy to the light touch of a finger.

5 When cooked, carefully remove the pudding from the steamer. Remove the foil and paper, place a warm plate over the pudding basin and carefully turn the pudding over and remove the bowl. (If you are not serving the pudding immediately, place the bowl back over the pudding to prevent it drying out.)

6 To make the orange sauce, bring the orange juice to the boil in a small pan. In a bowl, beat the egg yolks, cornflour and sugar until thick and light. Pour the hot orange juice into the bowl, mix until blended, then return to the pan. Cook over medium heat, stirring constantly with a wooden spoon, until the mixture coats the back of the spoon and the sauce does not close over when a line is drawn across the spoon with a finger.

7 Remove from the heat, strain into a bowl, then stir in the Grand Marnier or Cointreau. If you are not using the sauce straight away, dust the surface lightly with caster sugar to prevent a skin forming. The sugar can be stirred in just before serving. Serve the sauce warm or cold with the pudding.

Chocolate and chestnut terrine

This rich, chilled terrine is a terrific alternative to Christmas pudding for unexpected yuletide guests. It freezes well for up to 3 months. Serve thinly sliced.

*Preparation time **20 minutes** + **12 hours** refrigeration*
*Total cooking time **10 minutes***
Serves 10–12

185 g (6 oz) good-quality dark chocolate, chopped
90 g (3 oz) unsalted butter, at room temperature
90 g (3 oz) caster sugar
400 g (12³/4 oz) can unsweetened chestnut purée
1/4 teaspoon vanilla extract or essence
1/4 teaspoon coffee granules, dissolved in 1 teaspoon hot water
30 ml (1 fl oz) rum
good-quality dark chocolate, for shaving
fresh berries or orange segements, to garnish

1 Grease a 7.5 x 17 x 7.5 cm (3 x 7 x 3 inch) loaf tin. Line the base with baking paper, then oil the paper.
2 Place the chocolate in a heatproof bowl over a pan half-full of boiling water. Remove the pan from the heat, stir the chocolate until melted, then remove the bowl from the pan and leave to cool for 5 minutes.
3 In a separate bowl, beat the butter to soften, then add the sugar and beat until pale and light. Whisk in the chestnut purée until softened, then the melted chocolate until thoroughly blended. Mix in the vanilla, coffee and rum. Transfer the mixture to the prepared loaf tin, smooth the top, cover with plastic wrap or aluminium foil, and refrigerate for 12 hours.
4 To serve, loosen the sides of the loaf tin using a small palette or round-bladed knife; turn out the terrine and remove the paper. Using a vegetable peeler, shave off curls from the edge of the dark chocolate bar and use these to garnish the terrine. Slice and serve with fresh berries or orange segments.

Pears poached in red wine

A light yet satisfying end to a meal, this colourful dessert can be dressed up even further by adding some prunes to poach with the pears in the spiced wine sauce.

*Preparation time **45 minutes***
*Total cooking time **50 minutes***
Serves 4

1.5 litres heavy red wine
425 g (13 1/2 oz) sugar
2 cinnamon sticks
1 vanilla pod
1 clove
rind of 1 lemon
rind of 1 orange
4 pears
2 tablespoons redcurrant jelly
2 oranges
fresh mint leaves, to garnish
fresh raspberries or redcurrants, to garnish

1 In a flameproof casserole dish, bring the wine, 300 g (10 oz) of the sugar, the spices, lemon rind and orange rind to the boil.

2 Peel the pears, leaving the stems intact, and remove the blossom end using the tip of a vegetable peeler or a small knife. Place the pears in the hot wine, cover with a round of aluminium foil or baking paper, and simmer over low heat for about 20 minutes, or until tender to the point of a sharp knife, turning or basting the pears if the liquid does not cover them completely. (The actual cooking time will depend on their ripeness.) Remove the pears from the wine and set aside to cool.

3 Bring the wine to the boil, then reduce the heat and simmer for 15 minutes, or until reduced in volume by one third. Add the redcurrant jelly and allow it to melt completely, then strain and set aside to cool.

4 Thinly peel the oranges using a vegetable peeler, avoiding the bitter white pith. Cut the peel into very fine strips and place in a small pan with cold water. Bring to the boil, then drain and rinse well in cold water. Drain the peel and set aside. In the same pan, mix the remaining sugar with 250 ml (8 fl oz) water and boil until the sugar dissolves. Add the drained peel, reduce the heat and simmer for 2–3 minutes, or until the syrup thickens and the peel has absorbed the sugar and appears translucent.

5 Arrange the pears in a serving dish and cover with the wine sauce. Sprinkle with the orange peel, garnish with mint and decorate with raspberries or redcurrants.

Chef's tip For a rich, dark colour, soak the pears in the poaching liquid overnight.

Baked rice pudding

This classic favourite, so simple to prepare, cooks slowly in a gentle oven, allowing the rice to absorb all the liquid. The result is delightfully soft and creamy.

Preparation time **5 minutes + 30 minutes standing**
Total cooking time **2 hours**
Serves 4

750 ml (24 fl oz) milk
20 g (3/4 oz) caster sugar
2–3 drops vanilla extract or essence
75 g (2¹/2 oz) short-grain rice
5 g (¹/4 oz) unsalted butter
freshly grated nutmeg, to taste

1 Combine the milk, sugar, vanilla and rice in a 750 ml (24 fl oz) capacity pie dish or ovenproof dish, and leave to stand for 30 minutes. Preheat the oven to moderate 175°C (340°F/Gas 3).
2 Dot the butter over the mixture, sprinkle some grated nutmeg over the top and cover with foil. Place the dish on the middle shelf of the oven and bake for 1 hour, stirring once or twice with a fork.
3 Remove the foil and reduce the oven temperature to slow 150°C (300°F/Gas 2). If serving the pudding cold, bake for another 45 minutes, remove from the oven, leave to cool, then refrigerate. If serving the pudding hot, cook for a full hour, or until a brown skin forms and the interior of the pudding is soft and creamy. Serve hot with a teaspoon of good strawberry jam, or cold with your choice of fresh red berries or poached red fruit such as plums.

Chef's tips If the rice pudding is too dry, adjust the consistency before serving by simply lifting the skin to one side and adding a little cold milk.

To vary the flavour, use cinnamon in place of the vanilla and nutmeg, or sprinkle 15 g (¹/2 oz) sultanas or chopped mixed peel in with the rice before cooking.

Fresh fruit mincemeat tart

This mincemeat tart is made luxurious by the addition of fresh fruit, and is elegant and delicious served warm with whipped cream melting onto the fruit through the opening in the shortcrust pastry.

*Preparation time **30 minutes** + **50 minutes refrigeration***
*Total cooking time **45 minutes***
Serves 6–8

FRUIT FILLING
1 small Granny Smith apple, peeled and diced
1 small ripe pear, peeled and diced
30 g (1 oz) mixed peel
120 g (4 oz) raisins
120 g (4 oz) currants
120 g (4 oz) sultanas
120 g (4 oz) black grapes, pitted
30 g (1 oz) halved almonds
30 g (1 oz) walnuts, roughly chopped
pinch of nutmeg
pinch of mixed spice
90 g (3 oz) soft brown sugar
grated rind and juice of 1/2 orange
grated rind of 1/2 lemon
30 ml (1 fl oz) brandy
15 g (1/2 oz) unsalted butter, melted

SHORTCRUST PASTRY
300 g (10 oz) plain flour
150 g (5 oz) unsalted butter, chilled and cut into cubes
1 egg, lightly beaten
1–2 drops vanilla extract or essence

1 egg white
caster sugar, to garnish
250 ml (8 fl oz) cream, for whipping

1 Preheat the oven to hot 210°C (415°F/Gas 6–7). Brush a 23 x 3 cm (9 x 1 1/4 inch) flan ring with melted butter and place on a baking tray.

2 To make the fruit filling, place the filling ingredients in a large bowl. Mix thoroughly and set aside.

3 To make the shortcrust pastry, sieve the flour with a large pinch of salt into a large bowl. Rub the cubes of butter into the flour until the mixture resembles fine breadcrumbs. Make a well in the centre and pour in the egg, vanilla and 10 ml (1/4 fl oz) water. Slowly work the paste together to a rough ball. If it is slightly sticky, add a little extra flour. Turn onto a lightly floured surface and knead very gently for no more than 20 seconds, or until just smooth. Cover with plastic wrap and chill for at least 20 minutes before using.

4 On a floured surface, roll out two thirds of the pastry to a circle 2 cm (3/4 inch) wider than the flan ring. Line the ring with pastry, pressing gently against the sides, then roll a rolling pin across the top to remove the excess. Thoroughly drain the fruit filling in a colander, then fill the pastry flan using a slotted spoon.

5 Roll the remaining pastry to a 22 cm (9 inch) circle, to fit just inside the flan ring. Using a 9 cm (3 1/2 inch) round cutter, cut a round from the centre of the pastry and discard. Place the pastry over the mincemeat filling, pinch the edges to seal, then trim the edges of excess pastry and refrigerate for 30 minutes.

6 Transfer to the oven and bake for 30–35 minutes. Whisk the egg white until stiff, remove the tart from the oven and brush the pastry with the egg. Sprinkle well with caster sugar and bake for 10 minutes more, or until golden brown and 'frosty'.

7 Transfer to a plate and discard the flan ring. Whisk the cream until it holds its shape and spoon some onto the hole in the centre of the flan. Serve the tart warm and offer the remaining cream separately.

Chef's tip Be sure to drain the fruit filling thoroughly in step 4, so the tart does not become soggy.

Apple fritters

For a simple family supper, apple slices, tossed in Calvados and sugar and coated in a light, golden batter, are always a welcome treat.

Preparation time **35 minutes**
Total cooking time **20 minutes**
Serves 6–8

5–6 Golden Delicious apples, peeled and cored
140 g (4$^{1}/_{2}$ oz) sugar
100 ml (3$^{1}/_{4}$ fl oz) Calvados
300 g (10 oz) plain flour
2 tablespoons cornflour
2 eggs
250 ml (8 fl oz) beer
1 tablespoon oil
oil, for deep-frying
4 egg whites
50 g (1$^{3}/_{4}$ oz) icing sugar, to dust

1 Slice the apples into 1 cm ($^{1}/_{2}$ inch) rounds so that each has a hole in the centre. Combine 100 g (3$^{1}/_{4}$ oz) of the sugar with the Calvados in a small bowl. Coat the apples in the mixture and set aside.
2 Sift the flour, cornflour and some salt into a large bowl. Make a well in the centre, add the eggs and begin to whisk in the flour, then gradually whisk in the beer until all the flour is incorporated and the batter is smooth and lump-free. Stir in the oil and set aside.
3 Heat a deep-fat fryer or deep pan, one-third full of oil, to 170°C (325°F). Beat the egg whites into soft peaks, then add the remaining sugar and beat until smooth and glossy. Fold the mixture into the batter using a large metal spoon. (The mixture will be very thick.)
4 Drain the apples well and dry with paper towels. Dip single slices into the batter and place in the hot oil in batches to brown, turning to brown both sides. Drain on paper towels, sprinkle with icing sugar and serve hot.

Apple meringues with raspberry coulis

The crisp crown of meringue in this golden dessert harbours a smooth, marshmallowy interior. For special occasions, flambé the apples with brandy or rum instead of—or as well as—the raspberry sauce.

Preparation time **45 minutes**
Total cooking time **40 minutes**
Serves **4**

250 g (8 oz) caster sugar
grated rind of 1/4 lemon
1/2 vanilla pod, split
4 large apples
15 g (1/2 oz) unsalted butter
15 g (1/2 oz) sultanas, chopped
15 g (1/2 oz) mixed peel, chopped
15 g (1/2 oz) pitted dates or dried prunes or apricots, chopped
2 egg whites
250 g (8 oz) fresh raspberries
2–3 tablespoons icing sugar, and extra for dusting
lemon juice, to taste

1 Place 150 g (5 oz) of the sugar, the lemon rind and vanilla pod in a pan with 315 ml (10 fl oz) water. Stir over gentle heat to dissolve the sugar. Bring to the boil, then reduce the heat to a simmer.

2 Peel and core the apples, then add them to the pan and baste well in the simmering syrup. Cover and poach gently for 10 minutes, or until just tender, basting occasionally. Remove the apples and leave to cool. Set the syrup aside.

3 Melt the butter in a pan; add the chopped fruit and enough of the syrup to moisten. Cook over low heat for 4 minutes. Spoon the mixture into the apples and set them well apart on a lightly greased baking tray. Preheat the oven to warm 160°C (315°F/Gas 2–3).

4 To make the meringue, whisk the egg whites into stiff peaks in a deep bowl. Add 50 g (1³/4 oz) of the sugar, 2 teaspoons at a time, whisking well between each addition to form a satin-smooth mixture. In one addition, gently fold in the remaining sugar until just blended.

5 Using a piping bag fitted with a 1 cm (1/2 inch) star nozzle, pipe a spiral of meringue around each apple, from base to top, leaving a hole in the top. Alternatively, spoon on the meringue and lift it into spiky peaks using a tablespoon. Dust with icing sugar and immediately bake for 20 minutes, or until a pale, golden brown.

6 To make the coulis, purée the raspberries in a blender with the icing sugar. Pass through a fine sieve to remove the seeds, and add lemon juice to taste. Serve the apple meringues hot or warm on individual plates, with the raspberry coulis poured around the base.

Chef's tip Thawed frozen raspberries—or any frozen red berry—may be used if fresh raspberries are not available.

Chef's techniques

◆

Shaping quenelles

*These oval-shaped dumplings can be used as a
main meal or to garnish clear soups.*

Test the quenelle mixture
for seasoning by cooking a
teaspoonful of the mixture in
the barely simmering stock.

Drain and cut through with a
knife to check if it is cooked.
Taste for seasoning.

Form the quenelles by scooping
up some mousse with a spoon
and transferring it to a second
spoon, then scooping back and
forth between the two spoons
until the quenelle is smooth and
oval with three edges.

Once formed, wet the empty
spoon and use it to scoop the
quenelle off the other spoon
into the barely simmering stock.
Repeat with the remaining
mousse mixture.

Making chicken stock

*Good, flavoursome home-made stock
can be the cornerstone of a great dish.*

Cut up 750 g (1 1/2 lb) chicken
bones and carcass and put in a
pan with a roughly chopped
onion, carrot and celery stick.
Add 6 peppercorns, a bouquet
garni and 4 litres water.

Bring to the boil and let the
stock simmer gently for
2–3 hours, skimming off any
scum that rises to the surface
using a large spoon. Strain the
stock through a sieve into a
clean bowl, then allow to cool.

Chill the stock overnight, then
lift off any fat. If you can't leave
overnight, drag the surface of
the hot strained stock with
paper towels to lift off the fat.
Makes 1.5–2 litres.

Making brown stock

Roasting the bones gives a good colour to the stock and helps to remove the excess fat.

In a very hot 230°C (450°F/Gas 8) oven, roast 1.5 kg (3 lb) beef or veal bones for 40 minutes, adding a quartered onion, 2 chopped carrots, 1 chopped leek and 1 chopped celery stick halfway through.

Transfer to a clean pan. Add 4 litres water, 2 tablespoons tomato paste, bouquet garni and 6 peppercorns. Simmer for 3–4 hours, skimming often.

Ladle the stock in batches into a fine sieve over a bowl. Gently press the solids with the ladle to extract all the liquid and place in the refrigerator to cool. Lift off any fat that has solidified. Makes 1.5–2 litres.

Freezing stock

Stock will keep in the refrigerator for up to 3 days. It can be frozen in portions for later use, for 6 months.

After removing any fat, boil the stock until reduced to 500 ml (16 fl oz). Cool and freeze until solid. Transfer to a plastic bag and seal. To make 2 litres stock, add 1.5 litres water to 500 ml (16 fl oz) concentrated stock.

Carving a duck

Unlike chickens, ducks have little leg meat. Carving ensures everyone receives a portion of breast meat.

Place the duck breast-side-up on a chopping board. Steadying the duck with a carving fork, cut the legs from the bird with a large carving knife.

At each shoulder joint, cut the wings away from the body of the duck.

Moving towards the breast bone, cut the breast meat into slices. Repeat on the other side.

Bouquet garni

Add the flavour and aroma of herbs to your dish with a freshly made bouquet garni.

Wrap the green part of a leek loosely around a bay leaf, a sprig of thyme, some celery leaves and a few stalks of parsley, then tie with string. Leave a long tail to the string for easy removal.

Published by Murdoch Books® a division of Murdoch Magazines Pty Limited, 45 Jones Street, Ultimo NSW 2007.

Murdoch Books and Le Cordon Bleu thank the 32 masterchefs of all the Le Cordon Bleu Schools, whose knowledge and expertise have made this book possible, especially: Chef Cliche (MOF), Chef Terrien, Chef Boucheret, Chef Duchêne (MOF), Chef Guillut, Chef Steneck, Paris; Chef Males, Chef Walsh, Chef Hardy, London; Chef Chantefort, Chef Bertin, Chef Jambert, Chef Honda, Tokyo; Chef Salembien, Chef Boutin, Chef Harris, Sydney; Chef Lawes, Adelaide; Chef Guiet, Chef Denis, Ottawa. Of the many students who helped the Chefs test each recipe, a special mention to graduates David Welch and Allen Wertheim. A very special acknowledgment to Directors Susan Eckstein, Great Britain, and Kathy Shaw, Paris, who have been responsible for the coordination of the Le Cordon Bleu team throughout this series.

Murdoch Books®
Managing Editor: Kay Halsey
Series Concept, Design and Art Direction: Juliet Cohen
Editor: Katri Hilden
Food Director: Jody Vassallo
Food Editors: Lulu Grimes, Tracy Rutherford
Designer: Wing Ping Tong
Photographers: John Bader, Joe Filshie
Food Stylists: Amanda Cooper, Carolyn Fienberg
Food Preparation: Christine Sheppard, Jo Forrest, Kerrie Ray
Chef's Techniques Photographer: Reg Morrison
Home Economists: Anna Last, Michelle Lawton, Toiva Longhurst, Kerrie Mullins, Angela Nahas, Kerrie Ray

CEO & Publisher: Anne Wilson
Publishing Director: Catie Ziller
General Manager: Mark Smith
Creative Director: Marylouise Brammer
International Sales Director: Mark Newman

National Library of Australia Cataloguing-in-Publication Data
Winter. ISBN 0 86411 747 7. 1. Cookery. Winter. (Series: Le Cordon Bleu home collection). 641.564

Printed by Toppan Printing (S) Pte. Ltd.
First Printed 1998
©Design and photography Murdoch Books® 1998
©Text Le Cordon Bleu 1998
Distributed in the UK by D Services, 6 Euston Street, Freemen's Common, Leicester LE2 7SS Tel 0116-254-7671 Fax 0116-254-4670. Distributed in Canada by Whitecap (Vancouver) Ltd, 351 Lynn Avenue, North Vancouver, BC V7J 2C4 Tel 604-980-9852 Fax 604-980-8197 or Whitecap (Ontario) Ltd, 47 Coldwater Road, North York, ON M3B 1Y8 Tel 416-444-3442 Fax 416-444-6630

The Publisher and Le Cordon Bleu wish to thank Carole Sweetnam for her help with this series.
Front cover: Steamed orange pudding

IMPORTANT INFORMATION

CONVERSION GUIDE

1 cup = 250 ml (8 fl oz)
1 Australian tablespoon = 20 ml (4 teaspoons)
1 UK tablespoon = 15 ml (3 teaspoons)

NOTE: We have used 20 ml tablespoons. If you are using a 15 ml tablespoon, for most recipes the difference will be negligible. For recipes using baking powder, gelatine, bicarbonate of soda and flour, add an extra teaspoon for each tablespoon specified.

CUP CONVERSIONS—DRY INGREDIENTS

1 cup flour, plain or self-raising = 125 g (4 oz)
1 cup sugar, caster = 250 g (8 oz)
1 cup breadcrumbs, dry = 125 g (4 oz)

IMPORTANT: Those who might be at risk from the effects of salmonella food poisoning (the elderly, pregnant women, young children and those suffering from immune deficiency diseases) should consult their GP with any concerns about eating raw eggs.